Meals Around the World

Meals in India

by Cari Meister

W9-ACB-542

Bullfrog
Books

Ideas for Parents and Teachers

Bullfrog Books let children practice reading informational text at the earliest reading levels. Repetition, familiar words, and photo labels support early readers.

Before Reading

- Discuss the cover photo. What does it tell them?

- Look at the picture glossary together. Read and discuss the words.

Read the Book

- "Walk" through the book and look at the photos. Let the child ask questions. Point out the photo labels.

- Read the book to the child, or have him or her read independently.

After Reading

- Prompt the child to think more. Ask: Have you ever eaten Indian food? Were the flavors new to you? What did you like best?

Bullfrog Books are published by Jump!
5357 Penn Avenue South
Minneapolis, MN 55419
www.jumplibrary.com

Library of Congress Cataloging-in-Publication Data

Names: Meister, Cari, author.
Title: Meals in India / by Cari Meister.
Description: Minneapolis, MN: Jump!, Inc. [2016]
© 2017 | Series: Meals around the world
"Bullfrog Books are published by Jump!."
Audience: Ages 5–8. | Audience: K to grade 3.
Includes recipes. | Includes index.
Identifiers: LCCN 2016011647 (print)
LCCN 2016013040 (ebook)
ISBN 9781620313732 (hardcover: alk. paper)
ISBN 9781620314913 (pbk.)
ISBN 9781624964206 (ebook)
Subjects: LCSH: Cooking, India—Juvenile literature.
Food Habits—India—Juvenile literature.
Classification: LCC TX724.5.I4 M435 2016 (print)
LCC TX724.5.I4 (ebook) | DDC 641.5954—dc23
LC record available at http://lccn.loc.gov/2016011647

Editor: Jenny Fretland VanVoorst
Series Designer: Ellen Huber
Book Designer: Leah Sanders
Photo Researchers: Kirsten Chang, Leah Sanders

Photo Credits: All photos by Shutterstock except: age fotostock; 9; Alamy, 6–7, 8, 12–13, 20–21; Corbis, 5; Getty, 18.

Printed in the United States of America at Corporate Graphics in North Mankato, Minnesota.

Table of Contents

A Tray of Food

It is morning in India.
Time for breakfast!

Raj has a thali.
It holds all his food.

There is chutney.

It is a dip.

There is rice.

There is dal.

chutney

rice

dal

Raj takes roti.

It is bread.

He scoops the food. It is spicy. It is good.

He has tea.
It is warm.
It has honey.
It has milk.

Tia helps make dinner.
She cooks with spices.

spices

There is lamb.
It has curry.

There is saag.

It is spinach.

There are chickpeas.

saag

chickpeas

Everyone has a thali.

18

They scoop.
They use roti.
They use hands.

Here is kheer.

It is sweet rice.

It has coconut.

It has nuts.

Yum!

Make Kheer!

Make this tasty dessert from India!
Be sure to get an adult to help.

Ingredients:

- 2 cups coconut milk
- 2 cups milk
- 3 tablespoons white sugar
- ½ cup Basmati rice
- ½ teaspoon ground cardamom
- ¼ cup toasted, sliced almonds
- ¼ cup chopped pistachio nuts

Directions:

❶ Put coconut milk, milk, and sugar in a large saucepan.

❷ Bring it to a boil.

❸ Add rice and simmer over low heat until rice is tender, about 20 minutes.

❹ Stir in the cardamom and cook for three more minutes.

❺ Pour into a bowl.

❻ Sprinkle almonds and pistachios on top.

❼ Enjoy!

Picture Glossary

chutney
A chunky sauce, usually made with both sweet and sour ingredients.

roti
A flatbread made of whole grain wheat.

curry
A combination of many spices that is used to flavor food.

saag
A dish made of cooked greens, often spinach, and spices.

dal
A stew made from lentils.

thali
A big platter that holds little dishes of food.

Index

To Learn More

Learning more is as easy as 1, 2, 3.

1) Go to www.factsurfer.com

2) Enter "mealsinIndia" into the search box.

3) Click the "Surf" button to see a list of websites.

With factsurfer.com, finding more information is just a click away.